Stepping Stones to Self

Stepping Stones to Self

Journey your inner landscape and discover your original Self

eveline

Copyright © 2010 eveline

All rights reserved. No part of this book may be used or reproduced by any means, graphic, electronic, or mechanical, including photocopying, recording, taping or by any information storage retrieval system without the written permission of the publisher except in the case of brief quotations embodied in critical articles and reviews.

Balboa Press books may be ordered through booksellers or by contacting:

Balboa Press
A Division of Hay House
1663 Liberty Drive
Bloomington, IN 47403
www.balboapress.com
1-(877) 407-4847

Because of the dynamic nature of the Internet, any Web addresses or links contained in this book may have changed since publication and may no longer be valid. The views expressed in this work are solely those of the author and do not necessarily reflect the views of the publisher, and the publisher hereby disclaims any responsibility for them.

The author of this book does not dispense medical advice or prescribe the use of any technique as a form of treatment for physical, emotional, or medical problems without the advice of a physician, either directly or indirectly. The intent of the author is only to offer information of a general nature to help you in your quest for emotional and spiritual well-being. In the event you use any of the information in this book for yourself, which is your constitutional right, the author and the publisher assume no responsibility for your actions.

ISBN: 978-1-4525-0028-7 (sc)
ISBN: 978-1-4525-0040-9 (e)

Printed in the United States of America
Balboa Press rev. date: 10/7/2010

INTRO

Namaste

As we go with the flow of life, we find our SELF in an exciting time for humanity. Presently we are an honored witness and participant in a great critical evolutionary leap in history. Due to planetary alignments, our heart center is being flooded with Divine energies, inspiring us to heal our bodies, and deal with emotional blocks.

Political corruption and economic chaos bring us to a new vista. We no longer accept dogmatic thinking, no longer follow rules that don't apply anymore, or stay in fruitless relationships/jobs that lead nowhere. We don't accept through logical thinking, we are beginning to accept through the heart center; shifting from 'reason' as process of knowing toward 'highest source of significance'.

Time acceleration (higher vibrational energy) affects our body, mind, spirit ~ We quickly get exhausted & depleted. It is imperative that we embrace what is happening to us. We need to take the necessary steps to stay up to par with the rapid changing world; become resilient.

Now is a great time to explore the SELF ~ Journey through your inner landscape, and discover your authentic Self, the essence of your very own being.

Stepping Stones to Self is a collection of articles which helps navigate your journey. These are stepping stones to the essence ~ our duende ~ our diamon ~ inner presence ~ ultimate source of creativity~ the inspiring & enlivening spirit throbbing within.

(*) Author's personal addendum:

Nothing written here belongs to us. If there were any belongings, it would be the bond of LOVE with which have been tied many beautiful flowers of knowledge that are offered to humanity as a bouquet of service ~

All words are recycled ~ accentuated truths in favor of a higher truth ~ SATYA ~

This book is dedicated to Robert & Clemente de Bruyn for their ever present support ~ Om Shanti ~

~ Follow Your Heart ~

EMPOWERMENT from L.R.

The rare gift of eveline is more than explaining complicated issues in a clear and simple way. She is passionately involved in all her subjects, lives them first and thus is able to pass her experience on to her readers.

eveline also integrates her intuition and knowledge from the Knowing Field into her writings, surprising herself often by the accuracy of her words and its clarity, by trusting her abilities to be in tune with Higher Knowledge. She is a medium through which essential information is given and passing this on to her readers is a true act of love. Ultimately she writes from her heart.

eveline's articles are deeply connected with the body, mind and spirit; exploring all three of them in a way that transcends our dogmatic view on these subjects. Using the ease of a true seer she shows us alternative paths to walk through life and ways to use our body, mind and spirit to become one with Self and thus with All That Is.

By reading these articles one cannot escape the truth of the direct connection which exists between the body, mind and spirit, all is one, we are all one, so it raises our awareness to our own individual responsibility to care for all three of them. Accepting this responsibility, we accept the responsibility for life, and for Earth itself.

As eveline so eloquently points out: the earth, as well as our body, is a living organism, a conscious energy field, which connects with all other energies in our universe. We are here in this moment in time to raise these energies into a higher level by living responsible, aware and in conscious connection with the Universal Mind.

Thanks to writers like eveline we are progressing and growing as human beings. ~ L.R.

Contents

Introduction chapter: Highly Sensitive People (HSP) 1

01 - HEART CENTER - Shifting from Logos to Holos .. 7

02 - NEW WORLD - The Age Of Aquarius 13

03 - ORGANIC - Why Organic 19

04 - YOGA - What is Yoga 25

05 - SPIRIT - Our Spiritual Nature 31

06 - SELF - Honor Thy SELF..................... 37

07 - INTUITION - Your Intuitive Guide............ 43

08 - EMOTION - Show Some Emotion 49

09 - TRUST - On Trust 55

10 - DEPRESSION - The (dis) Comfort Of Depression. 59

11 - GRATITUDE - In Gratitude 65

12 - FEAR - Facing Fear 69

13 - LOVE - Exploring LOVE 75

14 - COLOR - Under The Influence Of Color......... 79

15 - SOUND - Sound Bites 85

16 - BODY - My Body My Self.................... 91

17 - GROWING PAINS - Letting Go 97

18 - LAUGHTER - Laughter is The Best Medicine? ... 103

INTRODUCTION CHAPTER

HSP: THE HIGHLY SENSITIVE PERSON

~ Beauty of whatever kind, in its supreme development, invariably excites the sensitive soul to tears. ~

Edgar Allen Poe ~

One in five people are born highly sensitive or are HSP - that means 20% of our population is highly sensitive. Being a HSP means your nervous system absorbs & processes ten times more information than an average person. Your nervous system is more sensitive to subtleties, your brain processes and reflects more deeply, you are prone to over stimulation, get easily stressed out and overwhelmed. Being born HSP interacts with experiences of trauma in childhood, due to being misunderstood, producing symptoms of depression, anxiety and shyness later in life.

HSP are born with special antennae to receive subtle signals. Though this is physically & emotionally exhausting, it is also a gift. HSP can comprehend faster, are generally more aware than others of beauty and pleasure, are better able to sense other's moods. HSP know what is needed to improve their environment, take greater delight in Art & Music and are conscientious.

When entering a room, HSP are able to pick up subtle nuances, sounds, smells, energy; sometimes even catch some lingering energy from an argument that happened before they entered. HSP are also very creative, intuitive, artistic and detail oriented; they have stronger emotional reactions, are spiritual, and posses a rich & complex inner landscape. HSP are loving and caring and feel a deep internal connection with people, animals, plants and the earth. Conclude that their spiritual life equals their physical life.

The darker side of this extreme sensitivity is that HSP quickly and easily loose footing due to loud noise, harsh light, chaos. Even particular medicines, foods, or smells can throw them off. HSP will need time and rest for recuperation often. It is important for a HSP to learn at an early age how to protect Self; HSP are, more often than not, extremely misunderstood.

Special gifts such as these bring with them special responsibilities. However, not many people are aware, and a highly sensitive person (HSP) rarely gets recognition. While a HSP needs more comfort and attention than the average person, unfortunately they often get pushed aside without being valued or getting acknowledgment for their positive attributes. HSP quickly get the message that things are not 'normal' according to the <u>ideal</u>, and develop at early age a negative self image. Many HSP hide their true nature and try hard to adjust themselves into our fast paced, loud and chaotic society. HSP will burn out fast and need periods of rest and quietude. Because of 'shame' infested feelings, many HSP live in solitude and therefor it is not a known fact in their circle of family & friends that they are indeed highly sensitive with special needs.

Not much has been written on this subject; many people are unaware and unable to detect and/or aid a HSP. Often when a HSP comes out with their truth, they are ridiculed and considered a nuisance. This shows that the negative aspect of HSP is more on the forefront than their positive attributes.

20% of humanity is highly sensitive. Different cultures have different reactions toward HSP; in Asian culture and Native American Indian culture HSP are regarded much higher than in Western Society. In Western society, outgoing, bold, extroverted personalities are rewarded, while sensitive personalities are treated as a flaw that can be conquered and defeated.

> *~ HSP's could contribute much
> more to society, if they received
> the right kind of attention. ~*
>
> *~ pioneer in HSP ~ Dr. Elaine N. Aron*

With awareness and education (understanding), much can change. HSP can live happier, more peaceful lives and develop deeper, more meaningful relationships. One negative aspect of HSP is that they quickly get into 'overload' mode, because of the many subtle stimulants picked up, from the outside (sound, light, smell) as well as inside (thoughts, feelings, ideas, memories), as well as energies from other people around them, which is mentally & emotionally exhausting.

> *~ It is usually the imagination that
> is wounded first, rather than the heart;
> it being much more sensitive. ~*
>
> *~ Henry David Thoreau ~*

Physical symptoms, such as blushing, sweating, heart palpitations, feverish feelings, will often turn into high adrenaline and tightening of muscles. The body then will go into 'fight or flight' mode and produce Cortisol (a stress hormone; the most potent gluco cortitoid produced by the human adrenal) which in turn can stop digestion, metabolism (causing stomach disorders), and other functions (bone & muscles get weak/fragile, cell regeneration is decelerated). This is the body preparing for <u>emergency.</u> This influence will result in internal confusion and the HSP will often times just 'give up'. Cortisol can also produce feelings of fear. When this goes undetected or gets ignored over time a HSP can become severely depressed.

ATTITUDE ADJUSTMENT

One of the first things HSP can do to move forward from this, is to <u>repair 'low self image'</u>. It is significant to recognize that we have the inner capability to 'cleanse & heal' our Self. Everybody does, not just HSP. There are ways to change thinking and behavior.

By training the mind to <u>move from problematic thinking into visualizing desires</u>, HSP step away from pain, fear and judgment. Embracing desires and needs, working on what makes a peaceful and happy experience. As HSP get older they find Self apologizing less about who they are, developing a sense of pride towards these <u>special gifts</u>. And when misunderstood, more able to walk away rather than trying desperately to 'convince'.

It is essential to realize that we are responsible for our own feelings and sensitivities, and that HSP learn to protect Self properly against societal ridicule, knowing that HSP are oft misunderstood and will not be accepted immediately nor unconditionally.

Health is defined as Inner Peace.

*~ Jerry Jampolsky, Author of
"Principles for Attitudinal Healing" ~*

It is vital that HSP learn to claim quietude to gather 'Self'. We can do this by being concrete about ourselves, for instance when in conversation we can say, "Hold on a minute, let me think about this." or "Give me a moment to gather my thoughts". This will allow time to go inward and breathe, to conclude what we are actually feeling. Effective communication is one of the most important life skills one can learn. For any relationship, and especially those with HSP, communication is <u>KEY</u>, and taking a moment to gather Self is a sign of strength and inner knowing (self knowledge).

It is beneficial for HSP to stay centered, balanced at the core, when coming into contact with others, as they are quick to let others' energy envelop and overpower their own. Build a strong centered Self by meditation and breathing exercises. Some other activities that have calming & centering effects are gardening, writing, painting, reading, massage, yoga, listening to beautiful music...etc.

A heavy load for HSP is that it is <u>impossible</u> to bypass the energy of others. When encountering angry people, full of negative energy, HSP suddenly become negative as well, and often find their Self agitated long after passing them by. It is therefor imperative to learn to protect 'Self ', to find ways to build resistance in handling such situations. Find neutral ground inside the heart, so that energetic information can be processed properly. A HSP who has a strong inner core, a strong sense of Self, will be able to withstand the energy of others.

Fear & insecurity is another pitfall of HSP. But if/when we change the labels around, in other words <u>start thinking differently</u>, we can embrace the signals as signs of change and we can show gratitude towards Self, for the capacity to recognise.

Note: When HSP are paired with non HSP, they find themselves less happy because they demand more depth in their relationship in order to be satisfied, reflect more and therefor worry more. They will also see more threatening consequences in their partners' flaws and behavior. Most people are ignorant to the reality of the drastic differences that exists among nervous systems. HSP are better off partnered with other HSP, as they understand each other better, and are more accepting of the emotionality attached to HSP.

Always go inside Self, and take inventory of thoughts and feelings. Accept 'Self' <u>as is</u>, and develop forgiveness and pride. Find ways to control emotion and balance at the 'core'.

~ Always find peace - Never dwell in fear or shame ~

~ Don't look for confirmation from others ~

Give your 'Self' permission to be, and love who you are!

01 HEART CENTER

SHIFTING from LOGOS to HOLOS

Our journey on planet Earth is to know our SELF. Staying true to our journey means never abandon SELF by compromising integrity, discounting intuitive feelings or ignoring the signals that come from our bodies.

Being loyal to SELF means caring for body, mind, spirit; reminding SELF diligently that at our center we are a luminous essence, capable of love & compassion. Here we find spirit residing with a healthy ego; one that is well developed, self confident, proud and unaltered by criticism and praise. The strength of which provides the energy for the stages (phases) of the journey.

Vibrational energy is changing

Currently more of us are becoming aware of the accelerated speed with which many changes (on various levels) are taking place.

Movements & alignments of major planets in the solar system indicate these changes. For instance, for the first time in 26,000 years the sun will be most closely aligned to the Galactic Center in 2012. The Galactic Center is the rotational center of the Milky Way > home of our solar system. This center is *the source of the most gravitational energy present in our galaxy.*

A planetary alignment called "Harmonic Convergence" set off this major shift in 1987, and bestowed upon us a 36 year window of opportunity for the human race to ***co-create*** a new aeon. A new era of expanded consciousness; an epoch in spiritual discovery. We are experiencing spiritual enlightenment through *collective awareness.* This transformation is evolution inertia.

A new concept of reality is dawning. We are understanding that the universe is entirely connected. Science now concurs; there is a deep reality in the cosmos, called the Akashic field, that connects and creates coherence. This 'Global awakening' is shifting us into a more HOLISTIC civilization.

HOLOS = whole (Greek).

HOLISTIC ~ emphasizing the importance of *the whole* and the *interdependence* of its parts.

This global arousal is moving us away from logical thinking; away from LOGOS, into the realm of the heart & spirit.

LOGOS = Latin for empty talk, a word, a joke, jest...

For us to go with the flow we need to synthesize SELF; build resilience, body, mind, and spirit.

This spiritual evolution into heart centered actions, is activated by higher frequency vibrational energies, due to the alignment of primary planets. Time is speeding up, accumulating momentum. This acceleration brings changes in our magnetic field, altering the endocrine production of the pineal gland; *our intuitive energy will be enhanced.*

To master these energies, we must focus our power and bring it into alignment with our soul's intention, appreciate the need for healthy boundaries and self control, while we build a pathway strong enough to allow this shift. The time has come to accept the communication between our heart, a cell and the galactic center, as programmed by the same holographic view of oneness.

What happens to us?

To reinforce this call for change our body and mind express disharmony. We have been taught that denial is the best way to handle uncomfortable feelings, yet this time we respond with compassion. Though any of the signals, including illness, can be interpreted as inconvenient irritants rather than intuitive feelings, we now realize that our *ability to surrender* will provide freedom from fear. Armed with the knowledge that our intuitive SELF is an aspect of our nature that will never abandon us, we explore...our need to stay in control, our need to know what is happening, our need to never feel pain.....

We begin to realize the reasons for the "darkness" in and around us ; the stress, chaos, collapse, earth quakes, tsunami's ~ and find ways to restore, rejuvenate. SELF >personally >> our community>>>nationally>>>>and eventually we start thinking global.

We know life to be a series of events, that teach us, through our downfalls, and thus allow us to grow spiritually. We learn, grow and become more and more aware. Through acceptance of duality (the cycles of death and rebirth) we create harmonic interplay between attraction and opposition. We now begin to recognize that we can take charge of our destiny, that when we think positive, we attract positive energy. We appreciate the prosperity that follows focused attention. We honor our heart's intuitive pulse, and are thus reassured that we are exactly where we need to be.

Everything is energy

To allow our SELF free flowing energy we now surrender ~ Let our spirit guide us. We don't loose contact with our *essence* or grow to fear it. We commit SELF to staying awake and aware, freeing us from holding back and allowing us to feel fully. Open to our passions, and those of others, we are unafraid to feel every thing. We learn to recognize the many masks we wear and realize that it covers our true significance. We no longer disguise who we are; keeping our energy pure. The universe responds to us...our dedication to SELF will make the difference.

Through compassion, kindness, truthfulness and awareness we have a clear perception of reality.

Experiencing the mind in a clear state we begin to *trust our instincts* and embrace spontaneity *naturally*. Our healthy ego will let us have strength in our convictions yet be open to others. We learn to use our *natural ability to access inner truth.* We believe in SELF, restoring the balance in our LIFE, our community and our world.

Find *your* SELF in the field of possibility, send out Love, gratitude, appreciation. Sit in silence, and wait to see what the Universe has in store ~

We know that through our actions we activate the law of karma. Realizing our potential, we learn to give that which we seek. In giving we learn to LOVE ~ in loving we learn to TRUST. Trust is what will take us to the next level. Trust that the Universe is friendly, trust that we make the right choices, trust that our love and compassion will enhance our neighbor's and so forth. Trust that peace & harmony will replace this ripped up, chaotic situation we are in.

* A new Golden Age is upon us. Opportunity is knocking. Collectively we have the power to aim away from political corruption & economic chaos and face global prosperity *

02 NEW WORLD

The Age of Aquarius - a renaissance of the 21st century

"...take your seat on the thousand petals of the lotus, and there gaze on the infinite beauty..."

Kabir

We are no longer at the 'dawn' of the Age of Aquarius. We have arrived. Currently a major shift is affecting all of humanity. Change is happening on a large scale, and it is happening at such an increasing speed, that it is impossible to predict the future.

As a result, many of us feel strangely out of tune with reality. We recognize that clinging to the old ways of planning life no longer works for us. We feel the need to get in tune with the energies around us; the vibrational energy emitted by the Universe. The main source.

For some, a drastic change feels appropriate; we might decide over night, to sell our home and move to another country or quit our job and start a new career. Others will allow (this energy) these changes to proceed slowly; maybe we begin to allow our Self to envision a new life or ask deeper questions that encourage us to discover our true purpose in life. This process is a natural sign of a growth we are going through 'en masse' and it is a calling of the Universe to have faith and trust.

REFLECTION:

a tool used to help tune out useless diversions so that we can tune into the voice of our inner Self ~

Changes:

The past few years have marked a positive change for humanity. It is imperative that we stay consistent and vigilant about our goals. We do this by concentrating on our vision. This in itself produces a complimentary energy to the energy emitted by the Universe. Nothing at this point will cost us as much, as resisting this inherent change. If we let go and empty our Self, we can let the Universe fill us. It takes courage to let go. But after all the letting go, we may find our Self open for, and capable of, new fulfillment.

With world events as they are, it is challenging to believe in a bright, prosperous future. All things considered can severely cloud the horizon. But the Age of Aquarius brings about revival of the spirit. Planetary cycles support the echo's of Martin Luther King and JFK. At the dawn of the Age of Aquarius, in the sixties, Martin Luther King had a dream of the promised land. A 'renaissance' and 'Golden Age' is right around the corner.

Hopefully we are becoming more and more aware of the many positive changes around us, as we are sliding from the age of Pisces into the age of Aquarius. A change of this magnitude only happens every two thousand years; the last time this happened, it coincided with the arrival of Jesus Christ.

Powerful changes sweeping through our world right now, facilitating a shift in mood, action and intention. With the age of Aquarius the human race becomes unified. We awaken to all our diversities and similarities, realizing a new elixir of spirit, designed by integrating all into one.

Evolution has brought us thus far. We synchronize with the energy of the Universe and our differences dissolve as we integrate into the whole. We are beginning to realize the impact of our interdependence. While a volcano bursts in Iceland, an earth quake in Haiti or a Tsunami in New Orleans, the whole world is affected.

"... my soul is in the sky..."
William Shakespeare

Pure LOVE

This era is one of peace, unity and pure love. It is about growth of our inner being; a growth of our hearts. In the age of Aquarius, we break free of axiom, integrating our individuality with our unity with the universal spirit. The present pulse, zeitgeist, is created by enlightened human beings who have successfully begun their individual journey within. This spiritual awakening brings us, the human family, true liberation of the mind; a synchronization of spirit.

These ages are "... celestial landmarks that guide to review and re-chart the future of mankind and planet Earth." and "...determined by the equinox precession, were shown to last approx. 2000 years, were named after the zodiac crossed during the interval. For each age there corresponds an aeon; the revealing of a new divine attribute. " (D.Costian, Ph.D.)

EPOCH:

> the beginning of a new period marked by radical changes and new developments ~
>
> c.6000 - c.4000 The age of Gemini corresponds to the flourishing period of early Hinduism.
>
> c.4000 - c.2000 The age of Taurus - governing this age was Krishna.
>
> c.2000 - c.1 B.C. The age of Aries - characterized by the establishment of the monotheistic Judaism through great personalities like Abraham (19th century B.C.), Moses (13th century B.C.), Confucius and Lao Tse (6th century B.C.) and Socrates (5th century B.C.).
>
> A.D. 1 - 2000 The age of Pisces brought the birth of Jesus and Christianity appeared.

Now we are entering the age of Aquarius generating a new awareness, a new spiritual order. Mystically, Aquarius signifies friendship and Pure LOVE ~

Personal knowledge that goes beyond mere words of others is the sacred principle of the age of Aquarius. To go beyond faith to find truth. Creed and Precept of the past will be over ruled and replaced by true faith in our Self and our knowledge. We will come to touch our own interior well of knowledge, and have faith because we know in our hearts what is real, pure & true and what is not.

The presence of pure love & possibility in the midst of our ordinariness is a response to the idea that our planet is sacred as is the desire to work together in ways that are mutually empowering and co-creative. We have been too unconscious to our inner life. This spiritual re-birth forces us to look inward for the tenets that uphold renewed ideals of love, honor and truth.

03 ORGANIC

WHY ORGANIC

*Every day is Earth day *
every hour is Earth hour*

Organic in short means >>> produced **without the** use of **chemical** fertilizers, pesticides or other artificial agents. Fruits and vegetables can be organic, but T-shirts can also be made of <u>organic cotton</u>, as well as 100% organic skin & hair care products, and cosmetics. Many more things are now being produced without the use of chemical agents. And it is a surprising experience to investigate the ingredients in your favorite product.

* Buying Organic promotes a less toxic environment for all living things. This includes you and the earth, and a whole lot more *

LOCAL AND REGIONAL PRODUCE

Organic food for instance, is higher in nutritional value (living nutrients), because it has a reduced rate of toxins associated with factory farming.

Our aim should be to buy produce as local as possible; this is a core value of the Organic Movement.

In addition to fresher food, and reduced fossil fuel consumption (due to less travel), the profit from these sales will most likely come back to the community.

There is a connexion between flavor and nutrition with organically produced foods. Food tastes better if grown at its natural pace, and contain no artificial ingredients. Organic farms use fresh water, quality feed, healthier pastures, nutrient rich soil, contributing to a superior taste. Organically raised animals produce a healthier product without the use of artificial growth hormones. Milk from pasture raised organic cows, for instance, has a higher level of Vitamin-E, Omega3, Essential fatty acids, Beta Carotine and other antioxidants, than conventional cows raised in confinement.

The use of ~ GMO (genetically Modified Organism)~ synthetic chemicals in agricultural production is astounding. Currently conventional farming includes an arsenal of more than 600 pesticides. Though these nasty ingredients will enhance productivity and increase yield from every acre, these substances create serious health disorders, ranging from premature births to behavioral disorders to cancer. Numerous cases of allergies growing each year.

~ Thank God men cannot fly, and lay waste the sky as well as the earth ~

~ Henry David Thoreau ~

ORGANIC COTTON vs. CONVENTIONAL COTTON
~ another example...

While organic cotton farmers use no GMO agents, 70% of the seeds of conventional cotton farmers are GMO, and even before planting are treated with chemical fungicides and insecticides.

Conventional cotton gets planted in synthetic (fake) fertilizer, requiring an enormous irrigation system (wasted water). Organic cotton farmers rotate their crop annually, thereby producing strong soil, which does not require any additional fertilizer, and retains its water much more efficiently.

For weeding the conventional farmer uses chemical herbicides, in multiple treatments, while the organic farmer manually pulls out the weeds, refraining it from coming back.

** Food4thought: 25% usage of the world's insecticides is accounted for by conventional cotton farming. So, even by buying an organic Tshirt you will save the earth! **

The 9 most common pesticides used by conventional cotton farmers are highly toxic and 5 of them are probable carcinogens. The organic farmer tries to find balance between pests and their natural predators, which is created by the presence and maintenance of healthy soil.

Before a cotton crop can be harvested, the leaves have to be removed, this is called defoliation. Conventional farmers have chemical agents for this process, while the organic farmer relies on the seasonal freeze to remove the leaves, sometimes turning to water management as a defoliation stimulant.

The use of pesticides, insecticides, antibiotics, synthetic hormones and genetically modified organisms (GMO) may intensify production, but at the cost of our health!!!

Luckily the world is making it easier for us to GO ORGANIC. Globally many Supermarkets have added a special Organic section to give their clients the option. And many Organic Supermarkets have sprung up over the last decade. Local farmers have started co ops and people are becoming aware, and making changes. Of course Organic does not stop at produce; there are many more products available in "organic" form than you might imagine. Explore on the internet and be surprised!

> *~There is hope if people will begin*
> *to awaken to that spiritual part of*
> *themselves, that heart felt knowledge*
> *that we are care takers of this planet.~*
>
> *~ Brooke Medicine Eagle ~*

Become aware of how subtle changes will not only enhance your life and make it more palatable; it also enhances your earth.

04 YOGA

~ WHAT IS YOGA ~

Many of us think of yoga as a form of exercise, and it couldn't be further from the truth. Yoga, a Sanskrit word from India, originates from the word 'Yuj' meaning to yoke; harness, unite. Yoga is actually one of six schools of old Hindu *Philosophy*, focused on the path to Self knowledge and liberation; a discipline applied to the development of body, mind, spirit ~

The science of yoga, designed to directly experience a higher consciousness, helps us to keep the body luminous, vibrant and pure. Hindu text establishing the basis for yoga include spiritual contemplations, songs & verses, spiritual aphorisms, physical breath work & poses and a whole lot more. In western society yoga is mainly associated with the physical aspect; the asanas (poses). In India yoga is associated with spiritual and physiological mastery, a whole system in which the asanas actually play a small, though significant, part.

> "...yoga is the path which cultures the
> body and senses, refines the mind,
> civilizes intelligence and takes rest in the
> soul, which is the core of our being..."
>
> B.K.S. Iyengar

SOME HISTORY ~

The history of Yoga is obscure and uncertain due to its oral transmission of the sacred text. Yoga originates in India, and although yoga focuses on the Self, it originally was community oriented. Sacred scriptures of Brahmanism called The Veda's, written about 3000B.C., contain the oldest known yogic teachings. Characterized by rituals and ceremonies praising divine power, they strive to surpass the boundaries of the mind. This is considered vedic yoga; veda means knowledge. In those days rituals, sacrifices and ceremonies were a way of making a connexion with the spirit world.

The scriptures of the Upanishads, composed over several centuries, further explain the teachings of the Vedas, describing the inner vision of reality. The Upanishads explain the *ultimate reality*, the *transcendental self*, and the **relationship** between the two. Taking the idea of the ritual sacrifice of vedic yoga, the Upanishads internalized it, teaching the sacrifice of the ego through self knowledge, action and wisdom.

Just as the Upanishads further the Vedas, the Bhagavad Gita incorporates the tenets found in the Upanishads. The Bhagavad Gita, The Lord's Song, stresses the importance of opposing evil. The Gita is a conversation between Prince Arjuna and Krishna on the battlefield. These songs and verses are a glorious story that tries to bring together loving devotion, knowledge & contemplation, and selfless actions.

The Yoga Sutras, written by Pantjali, a famous Indian Sage, around the second century, were an attempt to define and standardize classical yoga. Pantjali is often considered the father of yoga, and the book of sutras is a milestone in the history of yoga. The sutra is Sanskrit, and means thread, referring to the thread that holds prayer beads together. The

Yoga Sutras, Pantjali's vision of oneness, are composed of 195 aphorisms (meant to be memorized) with its underlying principle; Pantjali's eight fold path, the eight limbs of yoga.

A few centuries after Pantjali the yoga masters created a new system of yoga practices designed to rejuvenate the body and prolong life. Rejecting ancient vedic teachings they embraced the physical body as a means of enlightenment. With radical techniques to cleanse the body and mind, they tried to 'break the knot that binds us to our physical existence'. The physical/spiritual connection is called Hatha yoga, which is the most physical exercise of all yoga types, and is used mostly in western society. The word Hatha means sun/moon, referring to the union of opposites.

Hatha yoga is actually one of the main traditions of Tantra yoga; a holistic approach to the study of the universal from the view of the individual. Tantra yoga studies the Tree of Life as opposed to limiting to a single branch; all encompassing. Tantra yoga is a system which includes ayurveda, asanas, breath work etc. Tantrikas aim to expand awareness by identifying the factors that influence thoughts & feelings, and by transcending the obstacles. By refining our thoughts and feelings, peace, harmony & order can be created inside of us. We all know that to change the world, we must start with our Self.

In the late 1800s and early 1900s yoga masters traveled west, and the practice of yoga was slowly integrated into western society. In 1947 Indra Devi opened the first Hatha Yoga Studio in Hollywood, and yoga has since then generated a continual growing interest. Modern life has emphasized the material, external aspect of yoga, to the detriment of its deeper potential. Pantjali describes a comprehensive system of yoga in which the asana plays only a part. Unfortunately these asanas have been blown out or proportion, and make most of us miss the "WHOLE" point. Though the asanas are important, without the understanding of its value in relation to the whole practice, it means nothing.

> *"Freedom is attained when the mind
> breaks free from the confinement
> of the body and comes to rest
> peacefully in the lap of the soul."*
>
> ~ B.K.S. Iyengar ~

THE EIGHT LIMBS ~

The eight limbs of yoga are the core of yoga. It is an eight fold path that forms the structural framework for yoga. The practice of yoga can be divided into three parts: external (body) internal (mind) and innermost (spirit) ~ In the first tier of yoga, social and individual ethical disciplines are discussed (the do's and don'ts); Niyama & Yama, the first two of the eight limbs. The second tier leads to the evolution of individual understanding of the Self. We work toward this understanding through the body's interpretation. This involves the practice of poses (asana), the practice of breath (pranayama), and the practice of controlling the senses (pratyahara); the 3rd, 4th & 5th limb. In the last tier of yoga we experience and enjoy the 'wealth' of yoga, in other words the result, the fruit of the tree. This involves concentration and complete attention (dharana), meditation (dhyana), and union with the Universal spirit (samadhi). This last tier, the 6th, 7th & 8th limb, brings the experience of the sight of the soul.

YOGA TODAY

We are currently undergoing a surge of positive energy in the world. Many of us are becoming aware of the changes that occur in the Universe due to our own ignorance, lack of knowing. We are also beginning to realize the spiritual unity behind all the diversity in the world; it is our one connection. As members of one Universal Family, a lot of us are seeking harmony within. As our contribution we seek to attain our own 'natural state' of harmony & balance. We do this by watching our own experience daily and reflecting on it, noticing things and how we feel about it inside. This will expand our awareness, and broaden our perspective. It also brings a constant flow of new sensations and our awareness opens to infinite possibilities.

Self reflection promotes continual change and growth. Every day we are given an opportunity to adjust, tweak, re-establish and re-invent a new Self. While we explore the unlimited possibilities & opportunities it is important to keep our bodies in optimum health and keep our senses under control. We try to attain a calm, clear and well disciplined mind with a razor sharp intellect. We try to be strong yet pliable, while we walk with an open heart full of unconditional love and compassion. This is where our body, mind and spirit unite (yolk) and merge with the Universal spirit.

A tree has millions of leaves. Each leaf is different, yet they all belong to the same tree. We also have many leaves, our thought waves, actions, reactions, feelings, failings and restraints...but they are all connected to the same root of our being.

> *The practice of yoga leads us through the layers of our being, until we come to live and experience the ambrosia of the fruit of yoga, which is the sight of the soul."*
>
> ~ B.K.S. Iyengar ~

05 SPIRIT

OUR SPIRITUAL NATURE

*Spiritual awakening is no longer an
option, it is a necessity if humanity
and the planet are to survive.*

~ Eckhart Tolle ~

We are here on earth for the spiritual advancement of our souls; to grow spiritually.

Whether we are aware of it or not, spiritual growth is always happening.

Spirituality is our alignment with our higher self; it's our personality lining up with our soul, in harmony. It means developing the ability to 'go with the flow' effortlessly, keeping the energy of the Universe and our energy in unison. In this way we develop reverence for life, and stand in gratitude for it, delighted to be alive.

The essence of spirituality is that it reveals our true self. We stand in its bright light with humility and clarity, with forgiveness, love and compassion, not only for others but also for our selves. When we become spiritually sound (strong), we love our 'self' and our life, and thrive in it, because our spirit has arrived at our ultimate nature and purpose, connected to our metaphysical reality.

We are entering a time of higher order of logic and understanding that which comes from the heart. The heart is inclusionary, meaning it simultaneously comprehends in various ways. Understanding all that is, all at once.

> *Your task is not to seek for LOVE,*
> *but to find the barriers within yourself*
> *that you have built against it.*
>
> *~ RUMI ~*

Currently humanity is in transition, reshaping into heart centered behavior and beliefs. Here we learn that we are responsible for what we create. Being responsible for our own actions means working on gaining confidence and self respect; realizing that low self esteem is an excuse to be less than we are. It means consciously choosing our behavior, understanding that **we are in control**. Knowing that the inability to accept this responsibility is a result of insecurity; it means denial, and creates a false sense of self. With an open heart we should ask ourselves what it is that makes us happy, and strive for that.

Besides our current spiritual leaders, many artists and writers are leading the world into this new dimension of understanding. These are the people who are 'most open' to the flow of heart center. In a sense their art, be it a painting, a sculpture or a poem, comes straight from the wide open heart.

Often artists use their art as a vehicle for others to contemplate, connect with their inner Self and the world around them. Suggestively they establish a bond, interpreting and provoking feelings that are heart center based. Visualizing a truth; creating a transcending experience.

> *All major religious traditions carry*
> *basically the same message; that is*
> *love, compassion and forgiveness.*
> *The important thing is, they*
> *should be part of our daily life.*
>
> ~ *Tenzin Gyatso* ~ *14th Dalai Lama* ~

In order for us to grow spiritually, one of the first steps we need to take is to be open to the truth and willing to stand fearless in the unknown, trusting that we are capable. Reminding ourselves that on the other side of fear lies freedom. The spiritual path we choose does not matter as long as we put authentic energy behind all we do, and the only motive is to advance spiritually.

Currently humanity is crossing over to new spiritual territory. We are becoming more aware of the deeper meaning of life. We are synchronizing our heart, and using our heart to synchronize with our soul. All of life is synchronicity. All of life is meaningful. And currently the human race is becoming acutely aware of this.

> *Underneath the world of sense*
> *perceptions and the world of mind*
> *activity, there is the vastness of being.*
>
> ~ *Eckhart Tolle* ~

When we choose solitude, for instance in meditation, we come to a place of quiet and stillness. The world falls away and our external identity ceases to exist for a while. We become 'no body', and the pressures of the outside vanish. It is a place where we can stop 'doing' and just 'be'. We try to stop mental labeling of sense perceptions.

In our basic state of consciousness we constantly seek our Self; we resist, and run away from the 'now'. In meditation, or solitude & stillness, we find our Self more open, giving us a sense of awe & wonder. Here we surrender and find liberation.

> *Keep your heart in wonder at the daily miracles of your life; your pain would not seem less wondrous than your joy.*
>
> ~ Khalil Gibran ~

Spiritual reality is created by the harmony within spirit, body and mind. To achieve this harmony we have to find a delicate balance; learn to transform negative karma into spiritual strength. Spirituality is about recognizing polarities in life and death, in beauty and pain, in laughter and tears. All answers lie inside our heart, here we find our divine essence; the spirit being the direct connection to the divine.

Access your inner wisdom, and find peace. With commitment and self discipline we can build a strong foundation of spirituality. In finding our spirituality we find home base. A place to embrace the 'now', without question or further agenda; where we surrender and possibly find bliss. Life can be a sacred adventure; to pursue psychological wholeness, spiritual integration and fulfillment of divine purpose.

We must sacrifice our illusions of separation; we are all one. This includes healing on the mental, emotional & physical levels in service to the deeper revelation of who we truly are as joyful, loving, peaceful and compassionate beings; this is our **authentic self**.

Now is the time to embrace the challenge to become spiritually sound (strong), to transcend to your higher self. This will not only bring peace in and around yourself, but will certainly affect the people surrounding you as well. Become a powerful force in your own life. Tap into your intuitive, and creative guide, and realize your spirituality... realize life.

*Go to your bosom; knock there and
ask your heart what it doth know.*

~ William Shakespeare~

06 SELF

HONOR THY SELF

*"Every Human being is the author
of his own health or dis-ease"*

~ Buddha ~

When we look around we find a world in dismay. Unfortunately so many of us are suffering from some form of cancer, or from some dis-ease. Dis-ease, Decay and Degeneration are largely due to the presence of FREE RADICALS in the body. These are developed due to the accumulation of toxins in the body; a by product of our life style, diet, environment and emotional makeup.

Bringing the yoga philosophy into your life will surely alter this. Part of the yoga philosophy aims at developing attitudinal changes, that prevent the buildup of toxins through various practices and techniques. Yoga also has a variety of purification practices that aims at detoxification/cleansing of the body and the mind. This cleansing is important; it helps develop immunity by eliminating toxins, stimulating the mind, washing the colon>sinus tract>stomach etc., Stimulating vitality>(retardation of aging!), and increases awareness of SELF (thought, digestion, feelings).

ABOUT OUR SKIN:

It is important to understand and eliminate skin issues. Poor diet, poor stimulation of the circulatory & excretory systems and subsequent build up of toxins are the root cause of skin imbalance. According to the Yoga Philosophy, the practice of Asana's (poses), Breathing techniques, as well as internal cleansing techniques will serve to address skin issues.

BUT...let's not forget the toxins in our every day products, such as shampoo, soap, toothpaste etc. Commercial cosmetic & personal products are FULL OF TOXIC & HARMFUL chemicals which lead to a host of health problems. Some of these petroleum chemicals and synthetic products we lather up on our skin daily.

SUN LOTION

More than 84% of sun lotion with high SPF levels actually fail to protect the body, or loose their effectiveness fast. In fact very few sun products work the way they claim with the majority only protecting against burn, failing to protect against harmful UVA rays ~ the ones that cause immune dis-ease, aging, skin cancer...

Most sun screens lotions contain at least 21 toxic, hazardous chemical ingredients that can get absorbed through the skin into the body causing great havoc. For example oxybenzoneone, used in almost all sunscreens, can cause allergies, hormone disruption, cancer and cell damage. Chemicals like Octinoxate, octyl methoxycinnamate, chemical fragrance and propelene glycol are all toxic ingredients found in commercial sun lotions. Bad for us, bad for our beloved ocean.

START READING the ingredients list ~ www.cosmeticsdatabase.com is an enlightening & informative web site. The home page has a search box where products can be tested & scrutinized; each ingredient one at a time. This will awaken us to the many vicious chemicals we submit to.

Once we discover the truth about these odious ingredients, buying sun protection (or any product) with a lot of noxious chemicals simply will not work any more. It creates destruction in our body and in the ocean. Natural sun lotions, much more available now than ever before, are not only good for us but good for the environment, including our ocean.

> *"The goal of life is living in*
> *agreement with nature"*
>
> ~ *Leno* ~ *Eminent philosopher 335 BC*

Best kind of protection is what we put in to our body. Some natural ingredients (like green tea rich in polyphenols antioxidants) provides internal and external protection from UV radiation. Broccoli extract rich in sulphoraphane anti oxidants helps cells protect themselves...

Start reading labels and become aware. PARABENS for instance, come in various forms >> methyl-, ethyl-, propyl-.... anything that has paraben on the end is bad for us; they are dangerous chemicals. These are found in sun lotions, as well as deodorants, shampoos, moisturizers, shaving gels, lubricants, topical pharmaceuticals, tooth paste.....

PHTHALATES is another chemical that is in our every day life. It is a chemical used in making plastic (PVC) more flexible and resilient, and is found in products like toys, food packaging, detergents, nail polish....it can be found in any product; any thing that ends with phthalates (like dibutylphtalate) is bad. This ingredient is found in many body products.

Explore www.EWG.org (Environmental Working Group) - another informational site!

ABOUT PARAFFIN (wax)

This is a chemical preservative that is widely used for many reasons. For instance it is found in products like fruits and vegetables to retard moisture loss, and make it look shiny. It is also found in candy and often in chocolate as well. Please consider the fact that Paraffin wax is a heavy hydrocarbon that comes from crude oil. (fossil fuel).

What we need to do is look into using more products that have natural & organic ingredients.

With regards to protection from the beautiful life giving yet dangerous sun, we want to look for ingredients like Zinc Oxide & titanium dioxide for instance. These are physical "blockers" reflecting sunlight as opposed to chemical blockers which absorb the sun light, causing premature aging, skin damage, immune system damage...

Start using 100% mineral based sun protection, and products from companies that use raw plant materials. Products that are free from synthetic perfumes, colors and preservatives.

Begin by checking everyday products. Take toothpaste & deodorants. Here we want to stay away from aluminum and fluoride, artificial sweetners/detergents, SLS Sodium hydroxide....

Aluminum has now been proven to cause Alzheimer, Cancer, Lymph blockage, among other problems. And believe this>>>Fluoride has been shown to enhance the brain's absorption of aluminum. Fluoride also damages musculoskeletal and nervous systems, leading to joint issues, muscular degeneration and neurological deficit, and bone cancer among other cancers.

SLS is yet an other ingredient seen on labels all the time. (Sodium Lauryl Sulfate). It is a common ingredient in soap, shampoo, detergents, and toothpaste, among other products. It causes a variety of health issues. Once absorbed into the body it mimics the activity of the hormone 'Estrogen', causing implications with menopausal issues, male fertility issues, breast cancer.... SLS is the #1 active ingredient in many products. Look for it to avoid it. SLS enters the body and maintains residual levels in the brain, heart, liver and lungs... all from skin contact.

We can't expect our selves to go organic / natural overnight. It takes a commitment and a lot of research to make subtle changes. Explore and find out what works best for you.

Each of us, individually, has the responsibility to our SELF, and those who love us, to care and do our very best to honor our SELF by becoming aware of what goes into our body. We can re- create our life style ; excluding nasty chemical ingredients, and replacing them with products that have natural ingredients, that protect, rejuvenate, replenish.

Enhance optimum health, create vitality ~ for your SELF & for the PLANET ~ Nature is our best friend, honor nature, honor thy SELF.

07 INTUITION

YOUR INTUITIVE GUIDE

*For an impenetrable shield,
stand inside yourself.*
Henry David Thoreau

You are your own best friend. We've all heard this statement before. The sooner we can grasp the meaning of this, the sooner we will realize the truth of it. What does it mean to be your own best friend? It means being in touch with your inner landscape, it means listening to your inner voice, it means <u>trusting</u> your Self.

A sixth sense, spiritual insight, instinct; (the ability) to know something without conscious reasoning, immediate apprehension... pure knowledge>> INTUITION... the guiding light from within.

*The primary force is intuition.
In that deep force, the last fact
behind which analysis cannot go,
all things find their origin.*

~ Ralph Emerson Waldo ~

When it comes to intuition, the largest part of it depends on trust. Trusting Self. Allowing knowledge to enter your heart and trusting it to be true, keeping the mind and heart wide open. In meditation, for instance, you give the mind a rest and thus become more open to 'what is', without expectation or fears & desires. This is where intuition can give you room to grow spiritually, free from analyzing, thinking and reasoning.

Intuition is part of you, like your organs, and you cannot live without it. When you develop your intuition, and trust your intuition, your decisions become more fundamental and spontaneous. Trusting your intuition gives a feeling of freedom. Drugs, alcohol and cigarettes will impede the process of developing your intuition.

Quietude is the basic foundation on which to build your intuition. Regular meditation will strengthen your intuition; you will be more in balance it becomes easier to go with the flow of your inner landscape, and you'll not be bogged down by fear, emotions, exhaustion...etc. Know that your biggest source of wisdom lies within you; trust your intuition.

Taking care of self, body/mind/spirit, will enable you to tap into your intuition. Assume that intuition works for you. Trust that it is there to guide you in life's journey. Remind yourself that you are an intrinsic part of the 'big picture'.

> *The only really valuable thing is intuition.*
> Albert Einstein

It is important to pay attention to your intuition. Concentrate on what is happening in and around you. All your organs, your blood, your breath, all that makes up your life (your existence) works together to make up who you are and gives you life's journey on earth. It is this 'working together' that makes this happen in exchange with the world around you. Thus you are part of the "big picture".

The first and foremost step is to be aware. Awareness of Self and of life around you will give you strength in developing your intuition. Be responsible for who you are and for the actions you take. Decide your own path and let your intuition guide you. Self confidence will give you the (emotional) freedom to follow your bliss and will lead you toward freedom of restraint such as fear, dogma. Take the initiative to create your own life, give into the moment, and release your anxieties & insecurities. Experience life and the myriad possibilities it offers.

> *It is with the heart that one sees rightly;*
> *what is essential is invisible to the eye.*
>
> *Antoine de Saint-Exupery*

By developing intuition you build self confidence and will eventually live from the inside out. You will be able to control your situations and your emotions. You will decide what makes you happy and what hinders you, remove barriers, decide your own mood and eventually you will be able to enjoy each moment as it is presented to you. Once your intuition is strong enough, you will enjoy pure assertiveness, strong decision making abilities, choice, and above all a strong sense of self. Hence you will feel better. Your health will improve as well.

Meditation and relaxation are big factors in achieving this goal, and once you have momentum there's no stopping... you will be able to enjoy life as it is meant to be. Decide your own direction in life; listen to your heart. Animals posses intuition and we are witness of this every day. Tap into your own wisdom and realize your full potential.

Every artist dips his brush into his soul...
~ *Henry Ward Beecher - (1813 - 1887)*

For many people intuition is mysterious. Artists, on the other hand, are more familiar with the concept of this undefinable driving force. They tap into it (almost) subconsciously. We too can cultivate this non-rational way of being; rejuvenate ourselves, ground and balance our energies and deepen our relationships.

In order to do this we must learn to have awareness for the sensations that constantly soar through our bodies; these are signals that have to be attended to. In this way we begin to sense how they relate to what we eat, think and feel (etc.), and will bring our awareness back into a living connexion with our bodies & with the universe, experiencing the total 'body/mind/spirit' connexion.

This straight knowledge comes from our inner spiritual landscape, tapping into our 'higher' faculties, and is an expression of the soul. To experience this sense of bliss, it is essential that our emotional nature becomes serene and balanced. Regular meditation & relaxation, reflective thinking, and quietude are all methods to get into this state. It is a developed and discriminating mind that can lead us there. It is our 'higher' level thinking that brings us close to our inner essence of soul.

The only justice is to follow the sincere intuition of the soul.
~ *D.H.Lawrence* ~

The last endocrine gland to have its function discovered is the pineal gland. It is located deep in the brain, directly behind the eyes. It is associated with the 6th chakra ('Anja' or '3rd eye'). It is believed to be a dormant organ that can be awakened to enhance "intuition".

Rene Descartes called it "the seat of the soul".

This area is believed to be the connecting link between the physical and the spiritual world, and is considered the most powerful and highest source of ethereal energy available to human beings. This gland is large in children and begins to shrink at the onset of puberty.

The pineal gland secretes melatonin (a hormone) during times of relaxation & visualization ; when activated it becomes the line of communication with the 'higher' planes.

To activate this '3rd eye' the pineal gland and pituitary gland must vibrate in unison, which is achieved through meditation & relaxation.

Visualization is the first step in directing the energy in our inner landscape, to activate the 3rd eye. Intuition is achieved through 3rd eye development. We raise our consciousness from emotional nature into an illuminated awareness when the pineal gland is lifted from dormancy. We then loose our sense of ego and become conscious (aware) of our inner knowing.

Take the journey inside your Self and discover the 'friend' that will always be there, and has been there all along.

*We need to be willing to let our intuition
guide us, and then be willing to follow
that guidance directly and fearlessly.*

~ Shakti Gawain ~

08 EMOTION

SHOW SOME EMOTION

*Let's not forget that the little emotions
are the great captains of our lives and
we obey them without realizing it.*

Vincent van Gogh

Emotion is a chemical state in our brains which we experience as feelings. It is a very important aspect of our mental life, though often overlooked, and neglected by psychologists. A psychological state, arising intuitively (spontaneously) accompanied by physiological changes, involving changes that prepare the body for action. It is what gives quality and meaning to our existence.

*My duty is to try to reach
beauty. Cinema is emotion.
When you laugh you cry.*

~ Roberto Benigni, actor

Emotion is a response to events triggering bodily changes, motivating certain behavior. We come into this world prepared by evolution, to have emotions. The nascent emotions are sufficiently formed so that from the beginning of life we are able to alert others about our feelings. However, the path to emotional competence continues throughout life, and differs from person to person.

We all posses a variety of emotions, and have universally recognizable expressions of them. Robert Plutchik developed a list (1980) of eight primary human emotions: Joy, acceptance, fear, submission, sadness, disgust, anger and anticipation. This is called the 'wheel of emotion'.

Spinoza claimed: Body & soul are aspects of a single reality; emotions, as affections of the soul, make the difference between the best and worst lives, as they either increase the soul's power to act or diminish that power.

Emotions, a class of feelings, differentiated from sensation. They are feelings caused by changes in physiological conditions relating to the automic and motor functions. A certain perception (arousal) sets off a collection of bodily responses and our awareness of these responses is expressed through emotion.

Emotions have a structure consisting of biological and mental layers. It is a moving of the mind and soul. A response to stimuli that involves physiological changes: increase of pulse rate, rise in body temperature, activity of certain glands, change in breathing. This motivates us to further activity.

I am not interested in the relationship of color, or form, or anything else. I am interested in basic human emotions.

Mark Rothko, artist

Understanding emotion

When we put ourselves mentally into a persons situation, we can experience the emotions of that person more strongly (empathy). By learning to recognize emotions in detail, we can respond to them more appropriately. Emotions act to motivate us, by sending us signals, reflecting our inner landscape. By watching and understanding them better, trying to figure out our triggers, we can make better decisions.

Of the approximately 90 facial muscles, 30 of them have the sole purpose of signaling emotion to other people; in this way we even motivate others into action. Emotional arousal is a process of our senses. This typically happens when the body is triggered by something we see, touch, smell, hear or taste. The body then releases chemicals into the brain that act to stimulate our emotions, decrease cortical functioning and reduce conscious control. This creates physical agitation, and prepares us for action, be it a positive or negative experience.

A lot of decisions are based on emotion, especially those reactive decisions (as in a heated argument). It takes about 0.01 seconds for the rational cortex to get rolling, with the main driving force being emotion, disregarding and overriding logic.

Our ability to think rationally is hindered by our emotion. The chemicals that inhibit our higher cognitive capabilities and limit rational thought are the same chemicals released through emotion.

When we find ourselves in a state of depression, we are unable to feel any sense of arousal, interest & engagement with the world around us. Some people with Alzheimer, or other brain injuries, have an impaired ability to use rational thinking, because of damage to that part of the brain where emotions are generated, thus disabling them from making even the simplest decisions.

> *How much has to be explored*
> *and discarded before reaching*
> *the naked flesh off feeling.*
> *Claude Debussy, composer*

What we can do ~

Self knowledge is the first step to being able to handle emotions more properly. Become more 'emotional literate' ; recognize your own emotions (and that of others), identify and control them, then give yourself a chance to do something about them. Do not abandon them, try instead to balance emotion with reason. Take responsibility for them and for your (own) happiness.

Expressing emotion ~

Emotions are ambiguous, confusing, complex, multi dimensional and ultimately resisting of description. Emotion; the energy that empowers art, is a fundamental element in creating and perceiving art. Art provides a profound, lasting transformative experience. The essence of art lies in the expression of emotion, as well as feeling, mood, thought, attitude, and a whole array of attributes.

Art therapy is used to help people manage (physical and) emotional issues. By using creative activities to express emotion, providing a way to come to terms with emotional conflict, increasing self awareness, and expressing unspoken (unconscious) concerns. Other ways to learn to control (and express) emotions is through creative arts such as dance, movement, music, drama, poetry etc. This is the best way to get in touch with emotions. Creative art is healing, it helps to express hidden emotions, reduces stress, fear and anxiety. It also provides a sense of freedom. The act of creating is believed to influence brain waves and chemicals released by the brain.

Sing a song, pick up a paint brush, move your body to the sound of your soul. It will acquaint you with the wonderful releasing feeling all artists thrive on. This is not a secret, it is a fact.

> *I do not want to imitate life, I want to represent it. And in the representation I use the colors I feel and sometimes they are fake colors, but always it is to show emotion.*
>
> Pedro Almodovar, film maker

09 TRUST

ON TRUST

*True faith is complete trust
without understanding; it is to
accept silence silently.*

-The Tao is Tao-

As human beings we have been conditioned to think that we have to figure everything out ourselves, and as a result we have a hard time letting go. To accept that the Universe is abundant, and support that belief by having complete trust in 'what is' (the present), is considered radical behavior, despite the progress humankind has gone through.

The universe is abundant. In opening our minds to the concept of Abundance, and the Universal Law of Attraction, we can change and shift our beliefs around.

One great obstacle for many people is 'letting go', i.e. putting trust in the unknown. Often times when we seek balance in our lives, we strive to have things a certain way, to our personal perfection; most of us are not comfortable with uncertainty.

Change is an eternal part of our existence and uncertainty is part of that. Seek to stop 'overthinking' and start to believe in the inherent mystery of the world in order to create harmony in life.

Begin to realize and enjoy the challenges; learn to acquiesce to the rhythms of life and relax into change and challenge. This is beyond intellect and reason; it is something you feel.

What is important is to remove the barriers of resistance and fear, and to work towards acceptance and understanding Abundance; here the main component is trust. Look around you: nature is our evidence.

Somehow trust fell off the agenda. As humans our stories are that of struggle, control and survival instead of trust and collaboration with the Universe. When we engage in an ongoing relationship with the universe, we develop equanimity and grace as we learn to trust that life unfolds exactly as it should. This requires a deep trust.

When you trust that you are on a profound soul's journey, and everything that happens is in support of this, you are able to let go of outcomes and stay connected to the present moment. Surrender to the process of life, and you will release anxiety. When you trust the process of life, you can see challenges as opportunities to evolve spiritually.

As long as we search for security through dogmatic beliefs and material good, the 'natural way' will elude us. But as soon as we accept that there is no security through attachment, we will gain courage to go the 'natural way'. Greed will dissipate and be replaced with true compassion. It is our inner ego voice that keeps us from simply 'being'. We must gather enough trust to let go of fear so that we can turn off that voice and be still.

Our inner voice creates the sense that we need to control things, for we feel that if we were to just 'be', to co-exist with the universe, we could

*not trust ourselves; things would not
turn out the way we want them to.*
~ from The Tao of Love

Ego is the veil through which we see the universe. It is the voice of distrust. Although ego is necessary to be able to be a fully functioning, intelligent person in the real world, it also inhibits us and makes us fearful. Ego separates us from the universe and creates the fear of loss, which propels us to attempt to control life. Our ego makes us believe that if we don't control things we must live in fear of losing them.

Ego creates duality between our hearts and all other things, by separating us from trust in the universe. In protecting ourselves we have prevented our connection with the universe. We must lose our ego and learn to re-connect with ourselves; to feel safe and whole again.

It is not easy to recognize our ego and how it operates to make our lives complex. But the purpose of letting go of ego is to also let go of the constant fear in which we all live. We have been taught to ignore our hearts and follow our minds, when instead we should quiet our minds and let our hearts speak up. Losing ego will bring us closer to our hearts and will enable us to see ourselves in a different way. In doing so we will discover new dimensions of Self.

Accept that all experiences are important for what they teach us about ourselves and our world. If we can view both the universe and the individual along the dimension of time, we find that each of us has the creative capacity to represent the universe rather than be doomed to respond to it.

If we can re-connect with ourselves and with the universe, we can let go of the fear that separates us from each other, and find the ***pure love*** that connects us all.

10 DEPRESSION

THE (dis)COMFORT OF DEPRESSION

Your worst enemy can not harm you as much as your own unguarded thoughts.

~ The Buddha ~

The fundamental characteristic of life is 'change' and yet most people reject change. When change happens and our illusions of reality collapses, we often get depressed. Fortunately, as soon as we realize that illusions are just that >> 'illusions', it dissolves and the ego loses power.

Every body experiences life differently, depending on things like environmental stimuli, age, our state of consciousness and our social conditioning. We live in a consumer society, constantly allowing material goods to make us feel better; filling illusionary holes in our existence. Our reality has been constructed (conditioned) by harsh external input such as magazines and television.

We could be more grateful just to be alive and focus on what is really valuable: compassion, love, our health. Often times our hearts swell when we see a sunset, a moment of natural beauty; this is because it draws us back to who we really are, internally we experience a sense of connection and sacred alignment. We know this, and yet, according to a Harvard Study in 2007, almost 10% of the population in America experience major depressive disorder over the course of one year.

> *Your mind is your instrument, learn to be its master, not its slave.*
>
> ~ Nemez Sasson ~

Depression is created in our minds. The Buddha said: ~ "All things are preceded by the mind, led by the mind, created by the mind." ~ When we get carried away with ourselves and our lives, our ego, being strong and overpowering, takes charge.

Depression often occurs because of life altering experiences, such as death, divorce, or terminal illness. At this point we may feel overwhelmed with sadness, emptiness, hopelessness and loneliness. We have low moods, lack self confidence & self esteem, we loose our appetite, and loose interest in life. Exactly what the ego feeds on: negative energy.

Depression generally hits those who are unhappy with who and where they are in life, which happens when we gravitate toward what magazines and tv tells us is best for us. We have become a culture that grasps at sensory gratification, and have confined our selves to a material world. We have lost our connection to the inner landscape; our spiritual self.

We need to realize that the struggles and mishaps we endure on this plane of existence are the lessons our souls have chosen to learn in order to advance spiritually. We get bogged down by what happens to us, by what we don't have and think we need. But we really do have all we need. The Universe always provides us with that. It is a matter of trusting this statement.

We are all part of nature, like trees and plants, but because we have a brain, we have the capability to question our existence, and be unhappy about our life. We look for external gratification and find our selves more and more depressed, even as we reach and surpass goals we set for ourselves. Goals like 'I want to be rich enough to afford a BMW'.

> *Things are not what they appear to be; nor are they otherwise.*
> ~ Surangama Sutra ~

When we say that we are depressed, we may only 'think' we are depressed, which in turn causes a chemical imbalance in our system. Research shows that less than 10% of all clinical depression is thought to have chemical basis; by far the majority of depression are 'learned' phenomena. Low seratonin levels are a **result**, not a cause of depression.

Depression is actually a state of high arousal, with a high concentration of cortisol/ noradrenaline (a substance released naturally by nerve cells). Having a lot to do with the way society and life styles have changed.

> *Forget about your life situation and pay attention to your life.*
> ~ Eckhart Tolle ~

The link between what happens to a person and how they feel as a result, depends on how they relate to it, how reality is interpreted. There are many ways of dealing with adversity; a lot has to do with our thinking style.

Consider this:

All emotions come from thought. Learning to catch negative, depressive thoughts, and challenging them can have dramatic results. Changing behavior, perceptions, and thought processes are vitally important to overcoming depression.

One of the first things we need to do to eliminate depression is to **understand** that we <u>are capable</u> of changing our mind (and mood). This takes courage and intelligence.

Our limited 'ego state' can be eliminated by awareness. This is not easy, but self awareness can (and most likely will) lead to freedom from depressive thinking.

Awaken the subconscious mind; our actions and behaviors follow our subconscious instructions. Commit yourself to yourself, and put in the effort of positive thinking. This can be jump started by affirmations. It takes discipline.

What's really good for us lies right beneath the surface. According to divine law this deeper good is right for all concerned. We live in a competitive world, which leads to separation and sharpens the illusions we have about our lives. If we stop trying to appease 'ego', and crawl inside ourselves, we find a vast landscape of mostly uncharted territory. When we tread carefully, with open hearts and open minds, we may find peace.

Our task, then, is to expand our awareness, as well as our perception and our power to create. With commitment and self awareness we can penetrate the illusion. We can venture forth, step by step, overcoming resistance to transcend. We will find out that there is another life beyond the 'ego state'. This is where spiritual strength comes into play, which will lead you away from depression. Every step will lead you to new vistas that are real; a newly gained reality opens to a life wider and fuller. Resulting in more understanding of the beautiful deep meaning of life.

It takes a tremendous amount of investment. We all posses discipline, courage, humility and the ability to commit. We have to avail ourselves to these potentials. We have to be open and accept the challenge, and remind ourselves that we (and our minds) are constantly changing. It is the nature of nature.

Plant the seed of meditation, and
reap the fruit of peace of mind.
~ Remez Sasson~

A Buddhist viewpoint on depression is that of self centeredness; indulging the ego. A road away from this might be by helping others, such as the elderly or the infirm. Another way is to still the mind through meditation. Here the murky waters of Mind, left unstirred, become clear.

Silence is the doorway into the deepest experience of being. When we meditate emphasizing compassion and loving kindness, it may lead us to forgive and have compassion not only for others, but for ourselves as well. Remember: happiness is a state of mind.

Assuage the winds of your thoughts and there will be no waves on the ocean of your mind.

Harness the power of your mind, and create a life that is worth living.

Your answers are inside your heart.

11 GRATITUDE

IN GRATITUDE

*"Gratitude is the fairest blossom
which springs from the soul."*

~ Henry Ward Beecher ~

As human beings we have the desire to know our selves and find meaning in our lives, and we have the capacity to fulfill this. We are the only mammals that can reflect; observing thoughts, feelings, reactions and emotions. Every thing is our world is based on consciousness. We influence what we see. Once we observe, potential becomes reality. We create our reality with 'thought'. As soon as we direct our energy toward something, it will manifest. Being in gratitude will manifest a strong sense of spirituality. Gratitude wears a humble coat, and when practiced regularly creates a feeling of grounded and connection to reality. It stimulates positive energy and motivation.

Practicing gratitude regularly not only brings emotional equanimity, it also brings greater health and facilitates better relationships. Scientific study denotes that gratitude plays a significant role in a person's well being, and a critical role in the search for human happiness. While practicing gratitude, we become less stressed, less materialistic, and less depressed.

Instead we begin to live with more enthusiasm, optimism and determination.

From a world view, gratitude encourages a positive cycle of reciprocal kindness; one act of gratitude encourages another. We can increase our sense of well being instantly by practicing gratitude. It does not require elaborate rituals or a house of worship. Gratitude can be practiced anytime, anywhere.

> " *Gratitude is the secret to life.* "
> ~ *Albert Schweitzer* ~

Albert Schweitzer and Benjamin Franklin are two contemporary advocates of gratitude. Franklin even developed a list of 13 virtues which he reflected upon daily, evaluating his conduct. Genuine Self reflection affects many aspects of our life, both physical and mental.

Unfortunately gratitude is the most neglected emotion in the study of behavioral health. The characteristic of gratitude can be genetically determined, it is part of us. But another part of us is created by early life experiences and positive relationships, transcended as good things that are happening to us. Certain negative characteristics block this positive energy, such as entitlement and self righteousness, which will create bad vibrational energies.

> "*As we express our gratitude, we must never forget that the highest appreciation is not to utter words, but to live by them.*"
> ~ *John F. Kennedy* ~

Practices that influence us with a sense of gratitude is reflection, journal writing, writing thank you notes, prayer & meditation, even noticing ways that we are supported by the Universe. Gratitude is anchored in spirituality. With increasing material comfort, we tend to be less reflective. Now is the time to integrate gratitude in our life. Gratitude and appreciation create the most transformative energy available to us. When we consciously become aware of all that is available to us in life, and then acquiesce that gift, we release a dynamic current of energy flow of the highest vibration in the Universe, which returns to us in physical form. This is the law of attraction. Make gratitude a way of life, and appreciate what is. By practicing gratitude daily, life becomes more harmonious and we become healthier human beings.

> *"Gratitude is not only the greatest of virtues, but the parent of all others."*
>
> ~ Cicero ~

12 FEAR

FACING FEAR

*The biggest fear we have, is the risk to
be alive and express what we really are.*
Don Miguel Ruiz

FEAR: a distressing emotion aroused by impending danger.

We have a certain reverential awe for this innate emotion called fear; our survival mechanism responding to negative stimulus. What is at the root of fear? How does it influence us, and how can we change things?

Tracing fear I find myself staring at neurons in the brain. Its response is linked to activity in the limbic system; the brain structure that supports a variety of function including emotion and memory. Causing huge amounts of stress, debilitating our health.

FEAR: Ego based action.

Most fears arise from the mind of self grasping ignorance. Self grasping ignorance of the way things are; the root of delusion. When we are blind to the nature of our world, we experience fear and suffering. The source of this fear lies in our conviction that things exist 'out there', independent of our mind. When we see directly that everything is projected by our perceiving awareness, our fears will disappear. Things may appear as solid, real and independent of the mind, in reality they are as insubstantial as a dream.

When our ego is in control, our actions and thoughts are based on fear. When we stop identifying ourselves with the ego, which is no easy task, we find ourselves awakened to 'heart based consciousness'. Suddenly we receive glimpses of our true identity, our unique-ness; individually. Heart based consciousness is motivated by love. We are all multidimensional beings; we manifest ourselves in many different realities. Once we become aware that we can let go of ego based energy, we can let go of conditioned behavior.

Hopefully we can go beyond ego and get in touch with our greater self; realizing the multidimensional entities that we are. When we unravel ourselves from the grip of the ego, we may find yourselves in a state of confusion for a while. But we must find the strength to forge ahead, and deal with the raw, naked truth that gets exposed. Muster the courage to accept and understand its origin and allow it to be. Integrate tolerance in our attitude, and gradually we have created a new way of looking at things. Our ego has become transparent and we are able to understand our actions. Here we have to be prepared to look at ourselves with an open heart and with sincere interest. We have to be willing to accept who we are at this moment.

*** *Too many people are thinking of security instead of opportunity.* ***

Politician/ Author James. F Byrnes (1879)

We all have excess baggage that we need to plow through to purify our souls. With an open mind, and conscious of heart energy, we carefully tread the sometimes painful landscape of our past. We can take note and create room for understanding, particularly spiritual understanding. Buoyantly we will realize that we are master of our own reality and are able to accept and understand the meaning and purpose of our life's path. We will come to understand that there is an element of 'free will' present in everything that occurs and we learn about taking responsibility for our actions. When we accept our own responsibility, we are free.

Once we get in touch with the consciousness underlying our different roles and identities, we grasp the meaning of life on earth; we experience pure love & happiness. We can be playful with the aspects of duality and use it to bring creativity and joy into our lives. One important step towards getting in touch with the stream of oneness, the divine consciousness that is the undercurrent of all our experiences, is to learn to recognize the difference between ego based messages and intuition. The main thing to remember, while you explore self, is that genuine intuitive guidance comes from a place of love; inside the heart center.

UNENDING CYCLES

Consider the noise of ego and invite more fear; fuel the drive for control. Be mindful of the voice of intuition, and summon the flow of love. De-fuse fear and align with love; truly believe that the world is abundant and that you are unconditionally safe and you will be lead by the voice of intuition. You will be able to tap into your highest, true self. You will be able to step away from social conditioning and from ego/fear based behavior.

If you are able to allow ourself enough time, patience and love, you will find yourself fully awake in a moment of clarity in which new understanding is gained. Hence you will experience life differently and new possibilities are opened. Changes will occur in patterns of thought, emotion and behavior, which allows the possibility of spiritual maturity. It is well worth investigating.

**** Knowing what must be done,
does away with fear. ****

Rosa Parks, Civil rights Activist

13 LOVE

EXPLORING LOVE

*~ Love writes a transparent
calligraphy, so on the empty page
my soul can read and recollect ~*

~ Rumi ~

The degree to which you love yourself determines the degree to which you are able to extend love to others.

Learning to love your self is not easy to achieve; genuine self love is elusive, hard to grasp. It also needs maintenance which means constant re-charge, replenish, re-energize. One of the most important ways to love your self is to nourish and care for your body, by eating healthy and keeping in shape. Another way to enhance self love is by scrutinizing the way you talk to your self. Often times we have a tendency to beat ourselves up with our cacophonous inner critic. We need to learn to be kind to ourselves. This can be done by being aware and (re)adjusting/tweaking our ways.

You'll find, the more you love your self the more you are able to love others and the more others will want to be around you. When we love ourselves, we radiate positive energy and we become conduits for others to tap into. Your relationship with

Self is a pre-requisite to creating a successful and authentic union with another; it is the primary template from which all others are formed.

All the great wisdom traditions speak of the unlimited power we have within. Quantum physics and psychology both offer proof that our thoughts create our reality. Now is the time to move decisively toward nurturing and balancing your innate capacity for self love. ***Choose*** to believe that your life is precious, and ***decide*** to nurture and protect your 'self ', your environment. Self love is the first step toward this goal, it is the portal.

A new age has dawned in human consciousness. We now have knowledge and tools available to access healing energies. We can start making a difference **now.**

> *The fact dysfunction exists in our romantic, family and human relationships is a symptom of the dysfunction that exists in our relationship with life; with being human. It is a symptom of the dysfunction which exists in our relationship with ourselves as human beings.*
>
> ~ *Robert Burney* ~

To make a difference, we can start by developing a loving ongoing relationship with self. Remind your self that love is the **greatest source** of health, healing and growth. LOVE is inherent in **ALL human cultures.**

ROMANTIC LOVE

Studies have shown our natural mammalian drive; mental scans of those in love show a striking resemblance to those with mental illness. Love creates activity in the brain that hunger, thirst and drug cravings create activity in. Consider this.

> *For one human being to love another that is perhaps the most difficult of our tasks; the ultimate, the last test and proof, the work for which all other work is but preparation.*
>
> ~ Rainer Maria Rilke ~

Loving another human being takes a lot of self love and a lot of courage; we try to achieve an emotional connection with another human being. Often times we love, simply to be loved. Yet, we can find a way to love our selves enough that we give love without expectation. Here we find empathy, communication and a real & raw exchange of pure and honest feelings.

We have been so severely indoctrinated into the romantic myth that we have no awareness of the process of emotional programming that created this. Books, magazines and T.V. have trained our feelings into a delusion of romance. We all know that the divorce rate is out of control these days and how much 'depression' has become the norm. We lack a certain intellectual honesty. If we can abandon our cultural delusions and establish reality based relationships, we will get to know each other in pure form.

eveline

---

*No one would talk much in
society if they knew how often
they misunderstood others.*

~ Goethe ~

Communication is the principal building block of any relationship. This is not only expressing yourself properly and honestly, it also involves listening and responding properly and truthfully. A strong sense of self invites opportunity to reach the heart of any situation. Any person who lives with faith in themselves, who moves with self assurance and conviction, will tell you that it is not a matter of what happens to you in life, but how you handle the situation. How you think about it will determine what you do about it which will in turn build or kill your confidence. There are many common experiences in life that erode self confidence. But there are just as many experiences that can boost our sense of self. Self love is a pure & sure path to finding sturdy ground in this area.

We can create self love by honoring our selves, who we really are, and appreciating the process of our evolution; recognizing constant change and evolving into a powerful and loving human being. By remembering that our feelings are our personal signals. By appreciating, and responding to, the highest truth. By knowing that we *are* powerful and totally capable of creating joy and success...

*There is more hunger for love &
appreciation in this world than for bread.*

~ Mother Theresa ~

Love and honor your **SELF** every day!

14 COLOR

UNDER THE INFLUENCE OF COLOR

*I found I could say things with color
(and shapes) that I couldn't say any
other way ~ things I had no words for.*

~Georgia O'Keeffe ~

Sunlight is essential to all of life. Color is a manifestation of light, it has divine meaning. Color also has natural & psychological associations such as blue >sky > calm or green > vegetation> balance (nature). This is universal. Color symbolizes positive and negative. Color is all around, and is part of nature; part of life.

Color and light have a major effect on the body. For instance: blue suppresses appetite, it does not exist much in natural foods. Back in the day, hunters took the sight of food that was blue to be potentially lethal. The sight of food fires neurons in the hypothalamus. If food was presented in the dark, appetite would be suppressed.

Dark and light shades of any color convey different meanings. For example pink (light red) looses all associations of red (energy>fire), and takes on different connotation, that of tenderness and sweetness. Dark blue, a dignified authoritative color is different from light blue (sky blue/baby blue), which points to softness and ethereal feelings.

> *Green is the primary color of the world, and that from which its loveliness arises.*
>
> ~ Pedro Calderon de la Barca ~
> 17th century Spanish playwright ~

COLORS AND CULTURE

Colors have different symbolic meaning in different cultures. Green for instance, in Renaissance times, symbolised fertility, and was used in wedding dresses. Christians banned the color green since they felt it was connected to Pagan ceremonies. 20th Century America uses green to signify heightened sexuality. For the Egyptians, the color green is sacred and symbolizes hope & joy of spring. It is said that green is the most restful color to the human eye, and it is found to be healing and soothing pain. In China white is a color of mourning while Christians and Westerners treat white as a symbol of virginity and purity, using it in wedding ceremonies.

> *Color is all...it is vibration, like music; everything is vibration.*
>
> ~ Marc Chagall ~

COLORS & CHAKRAS

The word Chakra is Sanskrit for wheel and refers to the energy centers of the body. These energy centers resonate with the seven colors of the rainbow. A chakra is like a spiral of energy; it is an energy 'center' in the body. Each center consists of varying light wave lengths, creating individual particular energy. Each center is associated with a certain color. For instance violet, which is the shortest wave length is associated with the crown chakra, and red, the longest wave length, is associated with root chakra.

The colors that are associated with the chakra's are: Violet > crown, Indigo> brow (3rd eye), Blue> throat, Green > heart, Yellow> solar plexus, Orange> sacral, Red > base (root).

Color is absorbed by the eye, skin and skull, and our electro magnetic field (our aura). The energy of color has affect on us in physical, spiritual and emotional manner. Every cel in our body needs light energy; the energy of color has major influence on our whole (ness) body.

For example the (7th) crown chakra is at the top of our head. The color purple/violet relates to this chakra, the organ related is the brain. Some physical problems related to this chakra are mental disorders such as Depression, Alzheimer, Parkinsons. Some psychological problems are spiritual. Violet relates to self knowledge & spiritual awareness. The color violet is the union with our higher self, spirituality, higher consciousness. When this chakra is balanced, we show a reverence for all life, we are self sacrificing in service of others, and have a sense of idealism. When this chakra is not balanced, we show no concern for others, we display feelings of superiority, and there is a lack of contact with reality.

COLOR THERAPY

Color therapy is designed to calm and relax the body; to release negativity and to stabilize heart and blood pressure. It contributes to an overall wellness of the circulatory system. Color therapy is based on the fact that certain colors create a certain neurological effect on the brain. All colors throughout the solar system emanate light, which, banded together, serves as manifest matter. Matter, scientifically proven, is energy, and energy is vibration. Vibration manifests as various colors and tones.

Color therapy, also referred to as chromotherapy, is an alternative method to restore balance in the body, mind, and spirit. In color therapy the imbalance of the body is first identified, then, to restore harmony, a particular color is applied; a color that corresponds to that particular part of the body where there is discord (dis-ease). Some tools used with color therapy are lamps and color filters, gemstones, candles, wands, prisms, colored fabric, bath treatments, colored glasses. This therapeutic method can be administered in various ways, and is often combined with Hydrotherapy (involving the use of water) and Aromatherapy (involving scent).

With color one obtains an energy that seems to stem from witchcraft.

~ Henri Matisse~

THE COLOR ~ The three primary colors of light:

RED, the color of visible light with the longest wavelength, is the 1st color we see after the infrared band is passed. Red, is yang, thermal, heating & positive. It promotes cellular growth and activity, stimulates our will, and corresponds to our life force (circulatory system). It is indicated for colds, sluggish and dormant conditions such as pneumonia-bursitis-paralysis and arthritis. It is also a liver stimulant, an energy builder, and helps raise our blood pressure, increasing our circulation.

BLUE, on the opposing end of the visible spectrum, is yin, negative, electric, cooling. Blue light is often used to stop bleeding of the lungs, cure sore throats, decrease fevers, and relieve inflammation of the skin and gums. Blue is also used for measles, chicken pox, cuts, bruises and burns. Blue is relaxing. Soothing rays of blue light brings great calmth and peace to the worried, excited and nervous mind.

(*) Note: more dis-eases are treated with blue light than any other color.

GREEN is the color of balance, harmony, nature, neutrality and non resistance. It corresponds to the heart center, and heals illnesses such as heart troubles, decreasing & stabilizing blood pressure. It is also used to treat ulcers, cancer, head aches, nervous disorders, and acts as a general tonic (or boost).

The secondary colors are similar to the closest ray of which they are combined. For instance

ORANGE animates like red; this color is used to address inflammation of kidneys, gallstones, menstrual cramps, epilepsy and sinus conditions.

YELLOW stimulates the nervous system and the intellect. These rays have an alkalizing (neutralizing) effect which strengthens the nerves, and are awakening, inspiring, vitally stimulating to the higher mind, aiding self control. Yellow is used to handle constipation, gas, liver troubles, diabetes, eczema, skin problems, and nervous exhaustion.

INDIGO, the color of our solar system, is particularly beneficial in dealing with cataracts, glaucoma and a variety of eye issues. It is also used to purify the blood and the mind, to treat ear and nose problems, lung dis-ease, asthma and to alleviate mental problems.

VIOLET, the last color we can see before the light passes on to ultraviolet, concerns with neurosis, scalp issues, tumors, rheumatism, concussions, cerebrospinal meningitis, and mental issues.

The secret of success with this kind of therapeutic treatment lies in the knowledge of 'what' color needs to be applied, and 'where'. It is not to say that all symptoms will vanish. Color Therapy is an alternative method applied to alleviate symptoms; it is not a cure. Color awakens the energies of the soul, harmonizing body, mind, and spirit ~ in equilibrium with nature.

> *I think it pisses God off if you*
> *walk by the color purple in a field*
> *somewhere, and don't notice it.*
>
> ~ Alice Walker ~

15 SOUND

SOUND BITES

As soon as I hear a sound, it always suggests a mood to me.

~ Brian Eno, contemporary musician

GENESIS:...the light of divine creation was initiated by sound; "God said..."

According to most spiritual teachings the primary force is sound; divine speech set things in motion, divine sound being the cause of all manifestation.

Ancient rishi's (sages) conclude that the pronunciation of vowels correspond to the vibration of the 5 inner planets, these are: Venus (O), Jupiter (A), Saturn (E), Mars (I), Mercury (U). These divine sounds reverberate through the universe.

Some sounds are healing. Healing does not mean curing, it refers to improvement of symptoms & conditions. At last the power of sound and sound waves are recognized by scientists around the globe. Organized sound, such as mantra's and music, is currently used in many healing practices.

eveline

MANTRA'S

Mantra: the Sanskrit word for divine speech (among other things). A mantra is a mystical religious poem, an ancient formula of divine sounds, an energy based sound.

In the opinion of the spiritual leader of the Sufi order ~ Vilajat Inayat Khan ~ "The practice of mantra kneads the flesh of the body." With vibration of divine sound, mantras can help us feel more serene, invigorated and emotionally stimulated. According to Vedic belief, speech (sound) is the essence of humanity. Words produce physical vibrations, coupled with mental intention influencing the result. Mantras create thought energy waves, and are a powerful tool used by the mind. A mantra energizes prana (life energy), and quiets the mind.

One of the most primitive sounds is the sound OM. (ohm, aum) The Upanishads teach us that "...the essence of all beings is earth, the essence of earth is water, the essence of water is plant, the essence of plant is man, the essence of man is sound (reason), the essence of sound is divine wisdom, the essence of divine wisdom is the sound of the word, and the essence of the sound of the word is AUM." Here we learn that A, which vibrates in the lower part of our body, stands for the waking state (Vaishwanara) ~ U, which vibrates @ heart center, stands for dreaming state (Taijasa) ~ M, which vibrates in the head, stands for deep sleep (Prajna) ~ These are the three states of consciousness, the fourth state is the "self" (the essence of consciousness) which is present in all three states and also apart from it. The sound vibration AUM then connects the top part of the body with the bottom part.

The whole world, including our bodies, is made up of vibrational energy. It stands to reason, then, that we are affected by sound. Any sound. Quantum physics attest to the vibrational quality of all existence.

Tones sound, roar and storm about me,
until I have set them down in notes.

~Ludwig von Beethoven~

MUSIC

Organized sound such as music, can raise our inner being to a blissful state, and divine peacefulness. Clinical studies show the profound effect sound (music) has on our bodies, treating patients affected by Alzheimer, Cancer, and post surgical trauma.

My research and personal experience has shown me that music can stabilize our heart rate, improve our immune system, energize our body, lower & stabilize our blood pressure. Music can also produce endorphins, nourish our DNA, generate important proteins in our body (interleukin1&2, which stimulates disease fighting cells). Music improves conditions such as stress, insomnia, emotional well being, and a vast array of other conditions and illnesses. Music also improves learning and retention of information.

CHANTING

Chanting: a repeated rhythmic phrase, typically sung in unison by a crowd. A monotonous repetitive song, incantation, part of a ritual. Chanting stimulates energy in the body. Vocal chanting is particularly affective because the palate and the ear function as blueprints for the body's nervous system. Because of the rich phonetics, Sanskrit chanting is particularly beneficial; the complex tongue placements stimulate a vast span of energy frequencies.

*Words mean more than what is set down
on paper. It takes a human voice to
infuse them with shades of deeper meaning.*

~ Maya Angelou ~

OUR VOICE

Our voice is our own personal sound. If we carefully listen to the sound and intonation of our voice, we will find our essence; it will resonate in our body. When we stay connected to the sounds of our voice, the words, content and our bodies will be congruent. Singing is very liberating for our emotions. It liberates our soul. It lifts us up and allows us to let go completely. No matter if we sing properly or just sounding out vowels, whether we sing alone or with others; though when we sing with others the effect is astounding. Singing affects our mood, it affects our blood pressure, pulmonary functions, nervous system...our overall health, physiological and psychological.

ANIMALS & PLANTS

Animals & plants are also affected by sound. Bio mechanical studies show that the relationship of environmental factors, such as sound, and growth of plants is significant. In exploring sound stimulation it is found that animals and plants are greatly affected, much like human beings. Certain sounds help plants bear more fruit and can control pests as well. Dogs are subdued and chickens lay more eggs while listening to classical music.

Unfortunately, currently marine mammals face threats by natural and anthropogenic sounds. Certain sounds can cause marine animals to alter their natural behavior, preventing them from hearing important sounds. It can also cause tissue damage and/or loss of hearing. This is very sad, especially if we consider that the sound of whales, especially the mating sounds of the humpback, has a therapeutic & healing affect on us humans. This long slow sound, containing a range of pitches and repeated patterns, gives us a sense of stillness and peace. This comforting sound associates us with the tranquility of the ocean.

Luckily the world is filled with activists who are trying very hard to balance out the current lack of harmony between humans and the environment. We must try to think of what we can do to contribute to this cause, and above all we must pass the word so that we can create greater awareness. A step toward healing.

> *The only work that will ultimately bring any good to any of us, is the work of contributing to the healing of the world.*
>
> ~ Marianne Williamson ~

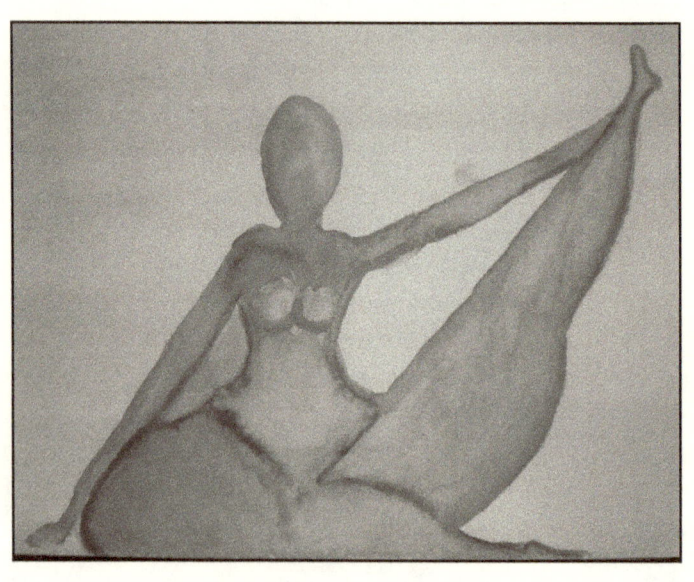

16 BODY

MY BODY MY SELF

*If anything is sacred, the
human body is sacred.*

~ Walt Whitman ~

BODY ~

The body is an integral physical material of an individual. The biggest 'collective obsession' is with the body. So many people suffer from low self esteem due to the way they look; from big super stars like Sir Elton John to ordinary people like you & me. We constantly compare ourselves to others, our weight determines how good we feel, our weight affects our relationships. Often times we are embarrassed about our body weight and find it difficult to undress. We find difficulty in accepting compliments and are forever apologizing for the way we look, projecting lack of love & respect for SELF.

Cultural focus on the body has been extreme. The media, fashion, cosmetic & diet industry all promote a beauty standard that does not come naturally. These advertisers make us believe that our bodies need constant improvement. This makes us obsessed with body image. The media portrays unrealistic standards that perpetuate social norms that are based on misinformation. (Did you know the average woman wears a size 14!?) ~ We participate in certain behaviors and hold particular beliefs that negatively re-enforce a poor body image. Many of us create eating disorders because of these negative feelings, living out a self fulfilling prophecy. Developing a healthy relationship with food and one's body is extremely important.

*You don't have a soul, you are
a soul, you have a body.*

~ C.S. Lewis ~

Our body is the vessel of our soul. With self love & self respect we can banish these old beliefs and create a 'high opinion' of the body. Consider this: The body consists of trillions of cells. These cells are all working together for the maintenance of the entire organism (the body). There are varied processes by which the body internally regulates itself. These processes need constant feedback > our thoughts! Sustainable systems require a combination of positive & negative feedback.

Dis-ease and cellular malfunction is caused by either a deficiency (cells not getting what they need; improper nourishment) or toxicity (cells being poisoned; alcohol, drugs etc.) ~ In addition to the internal control (our thoughts) there are external influences as well (Life style, environment etc.) ~ Our body is our temple and we have to ensure its optimum condition. We owe it to ourselves and yet some times it seems impossible to have the discipline to be diligent, especially when times are tough, and self esteem is absent.

BE RESPONSIBLE ~

Responsibility stands as one of the highest spiritual qualities, and begins with our body. We have to take the responsibility to feel good about our SELF. The body offers a fertile arena for inner work. Instinctive intuition of what our body really needs challenges our perceptions and fixed opinions. Awareness grounds us in present moment and provides a necessary platform for deeper spirituality. As a proper object for our love & respect, a cared for body repays us with well being, energy and a home for building our soul.

Closely connected to the body is the mind (ego). It takes discipline and diligence to re-wire & re-program the mind. Self esteem is one of the biggest factors here. Negative, adverse, threatening events evoke strong and rapid physiological, cognitive, emotional, behavioral, and social responses. Emotions (worry, upset, anxiety) chemically affect the body on almost every level; even imagined events can stimulate a response. Often times a negative event will trigger a lowering of self esteem acted out in poor care of SELF (the body).

When we feel overwhelmed with what to do about an issue/situation, or see no resolution, we begin to focus on our Self, labeling the problem to be with us (and often our weight). All this mental programming, by the fashion and weight loss industry, created a very unhealthy obsession in our society.

Our sense of our own body is the most primal experience. Research shows this 'sense' is prone to psychological distortion that can have profound affect on how we view ourselves. According to a study by U of Penn, women tend to distort their perceptions of their bodies negatively, while men distort their perceptions in a more positive self aggrandizing way (equally bad). It is important to realize the powerful impact of the 'immediate experience' of one's body in every situation. Body image is crucial to a person's sense of SELF.

> *There is a constant process of feeling
> one's body is growing larger & smaller, as
> different life conditions are encountered.*
>
> *Dr. Fisher ~ body image theorist*

One of the main factors researchers propose as giving us a skewed sense of the 'ideal' body is the extremely thin models used at fashion shows and advertisements.

> *The body is your temple, keep it pure
> & clean for the soul to reside in.*
>
> *~ B.K.S. Iyengar ~*

THE PROBLEM ~

Bad body thoughts are the culprit. The problem lies in the fact that we allow other people's opinions to dictate how we should feel about our bodies and our SELF. Our self image is created by the messages we get from outside of us: media, friends, entertainment industry, our parents; our relentless ego slowly hammering at our self esteem.

THE SOLUTION

We can learn to re-align our thoughts. Awareness is key! As soon as we realize a negative 'body thought' we can pull back from that by challenging that thought, by thinking kind thoughts about out bodies, by accepting 'self' with compassion and by putting focus on what is really the issue (family, work, relationship etc.). We need to remind ourselves that we are being unrealistic.

HOW ~

What to do? Accept our SELF the way we are, and realize that weight loss has no baring on our intelligence nor our personality. Take the focus off the areas we dislike and bring them to the areas we do like. Practice self affirmations daily. Dress to express, not to impress. Stay away from the scale. It is important to notice nice things about our selves and our bodies. Stay alert to fight negative self talk. Stay active and involved with SELF. Realize & respect the relationship we have with SELF.

There is beauty in every one.

A NEW WORLD ~

Create your own world. Embrace the unique SELF. We are free to invent a life that excites us. An abundant life that inspires us, a life we enjoy. Choose to see the beauty in your Self. Imagine the myriad possibilities, freed from rules, pressures and self punishments. Think of the body as the vehicle for dreams, and respect it. There is so much beauty in each of us; become conscious, awake and aware.

Na Hanyate Hamyamane Sarire

*Consciousness is eternal; it is not
vanquished with the destruction
of the temporary body.*

~ Bhagavad Gita ~

17 GROWING PAINS

LETTING GO

> *He's gone! The one I'm never
> tired of. No cure for my broken
> heart. The rose has lost its petals,
> but the thorn is left behind.*
>
> ~ Rumi ~

These days divorce rate is incredibly high; a lot of us are left with a broken heart. A lot of us, too, have a hard time letting go of the past and moving on. Disappointed we search, grasping at self help books, filling our minds with new theories, new methods and new ways of learning to stand alone. It is very hard to let go of the past, especially if you have been let down and your ego is bruised, your self esteem is at an all time low and your motivation is shot. What then, are we to do without the strength to move forward. Angry and disappointed we are prone to depression, loosing our way even more. Some of us try it alone, claiming that we don't need anybody and shutting ourselves off to the love and affection from our friends and family. Some of us dive into food, alcohol and drugs, numbing our hearts and closing the gates to our soul.

What are we supposed to do?

Spirituality brings one back to reality, gives strength to move on, and helps to put balance in life. Meditation, leaning into the moment, learning to accept truth, as it is presented, hoping to glean the hidden lessons. Nutrition is also a big factor. But, the biggest and foremost factor involved is a serious commitment to Self, and an enormous amount of discipline.

> *Renunciation is not 'getting rid of the things in this world', but accepting that they pass away."*
>
> *Aitken Roshi ~*

STEPPING STONES

There are steps on this road to recovery. The first would be awareness; to comprehend that **we can not control** each other or situations, and recognize the **potential for spiritual growth** in each painful situation. By accepting that things are as they are, we can develop discipline, patience and our threshold for tolerance. In this transformation we will change our attitude, arriving at a higher level thinking. When using our higher level faculties we begin to realize the clinging pattern. We are clinging to our negativity and fears, which is useless, destructive, ego based behavior; it is self pity. If we can recognize this truth, we will realize that change <u>has</u> to take place.

At this point we understand that we are not our feelings, though we cling to them, and realize that we are 'capable' of change. Visualization is a good place to start: holding the negative emotions in your hands and imagine squeezing them out, releasing them, letting them go.

THERE'S MORE...

But there's more to letting go than recognition, validation of 'what is' and visualization of letting the pain subside and vanish. The discipline lies in moving on from this point. Continual positive thinking is important in moving forward.

We can start by using affirmations.

Some affirmations are directly connected to the chakras. When the heart is full, focus on the (4th) heart chakra, where our 'right to love' exists. I am worthy of love ~ I am loving to myself and others ~ There is an infinity supply of love ~ I live in balance with others. The color green is associated with the heart center; wearing something green strengthens your affirmations. To focus on intuition, located at the third eye center, the 6th chakra,where the 'right to see' dwells we affirm, "I see al things in clarity. I am open to the wisdom within. I can manifest my vision...". Light indigo is the associated color.

Affirming also lies in the *acknowlegment* of the interdependence of all things with the divine, and *becoming cognizant* of surrounding energies. Honor Self and move in the right direction.

> The promises of this world are for the most
> part vain phantoms; to confide in one's
> self, and become something of worth
> and value is the best and safest course.
>
> ~ Michael Angelo ~

We want to be able to meet life's challenges; be role models for our peers and children, committed to leading a productive life, contributing to the whole. I am reminded often of the "four agreements" that has been developed by the Toltec wisdom, and has been passed down to us by Don Miguel Ruiz, in his book of the same title. These agreements are simple to remember, and when put into practice, certainly brings one to a beautiful plateau. The four agreements are: 1) Speak only the the truth. 2) Don't take anything personally. 3) Do not assume. 4) Always do your best.

There is so much diverse wisdom from which to choose at this moment in time. We are blessed, to live in a time where it is more acceptable to 'find your own way' and where there is a vast wealth of spiritual information from which to draw *that which speaks loudest in our heart.*

Another example of simple rules to live by, is the 5 aspects of Buddhism:

1) All I have are my actions. 2) Develop a fearless compassion for suffering, including your own. 3) Nothing is permanent. 4) There's no escape from illness and death. 5) Find refuge within; through mindfulness of thought, sensation and attachment.

> *Who has not sat, afraid, before*
> *his own heart's curtain?*
>
> ~Rainer Maria Rilke~

SELFto Self

Your dedication to yourself is what will make the difference. Diligent creation of positive thinking will move you to a different place, where suddenly more awake and aware, you will find yourself free from holding back and able to fully 'feel'. Our journey is to know our 'self '. We can move to a place where we can look at ourselves without submission to false beliefs, without masks that block our connexions to our perfect essence. Here we find forgiveness for those that hurt us and for ourselves. We see that at the center we are a luminous essence, capable of love and compassion.

When we stay true to our personal journey, we do not abandon 'self' by compromising our integrity or discount our intuition. We remain contact with our essence and not grow to fear it. We stay loyal to our journey, and not disguise who we really are, keeping our essence pure. By letting go and moving on we don't get invested in negativity nor yield to false beliefs, which puts limits on the free flow of energy in our bodies. We feel liberated from constraint.

Remind yourself that everything is energy; surrender to it, let it take you. Stay open to feeling every thing, open and unafraid. Taking a leap of faith into the unknown will reveal your true self. It will enable you to truly stay in the moment and let go of all that is holding you down.

> *Almost always it is the fear of being ourselves that brings us to the mirror.*
>
> ~ *Antonio Porchia* ~ *(Italian Poet ~ 1885~1968)*

18 LAUGHTER

LAUGHTER IS THE BEST MEDICINE?

*The most wasted of all days,
is one without laughter.*

e.e.cummings ~

Although some of us take it for granted, laughter is an intrinsic, fundamental part of our lives. Research shows that laughing is a 'full cortex' experience, meaning that before we laugh, an electrical wave (current) sweeps through and completely blankets the cortex.

Laughter has wide ranging effects, physiologically as well as psychologically After a laugh, the blood pressure and heart rate go below normal, putting the body into a relaxed state, closer to the pulse of Earth. Additionally it, indirectly, stimulates endorphins, which is a natural pain killer. Laughter increases creative thinking, encouraging out of ordinary ways of looking at things.

Scientifically, laughter activates T-lymphocytes and natural killer cells, both of which destroy invading micro organisms. It also increases production of immunity boosting gamma interferon (essential for resistance to viral infections), and speeds up the production of new immune cells. Laughter **reduces** levels of the stress hormone 'cortisol', which weakens the immune response; and affects the levels of immunoglobulin-A, an anti body secreted in saliva to **protect** against respiratory invaders.

Humor may help some people more than others. Nearly all research links mood with humor, this is called correlational, hence the more sober minded may benefit less from laughter. It is therefor important that we learn to put ourselves into a more playful state of mind.

LAUGHTER:

alleviates depression, lowers blood pressure, improves blood circulation, causes the body to secrete enzymes that protect the body from forming an ulcer, it promotes relaxation, reduces stress, and gives more energy by increasing oxygen levels in the blood.

> *At the height of laughter, the universe is flung into a kaleidoscope of new possibilities.*
> Jean Houston ~

Humor is intensely personal. This instinctual development occurs very early in life. As a motor reflex, laughter usually presents itself four months after birth. There are reports that claim that children laugh approximately 400 times day, if we let them! Adults on the other hand laugh about 15 times a day, if they're lucky. Perhaps the children in our lives can show us the way back to laughter.

Humor is a very important ingredient in a relationship. Not only is it a powerful and reliable way to show talent and creativity, wit also reveals an active and healthy brain; it is a powerful antidote to severe problems, and a major attracting force.

Unfortunately, a lot of people see humor as superficial, which is why some people are so reserved. Yet, humor is important in working through problems. We have to incorporate humor into our lives more. We can train ourselves to think more optimistically, enthusiastically. If we do this often enough, we easily change negative experiences into something positive.

When we learn to take ourselves less serious, break away from conventional expectations, give life a creative twist, we find our relationship with Self and with others bounteous, our health enhanced, and a happier human being. This benefits not only our selves, but those around us as well.

Laughter is the shortest distance between two people.
Victor Borge ~

(*) ~ On a personal note: Some years ago my sweet Paul got struck with AIDS, through him I learned that laughter is a very powerful antidote. I witnessed how his sense of humor literally added years to his life. I dedicate this article to Paulie, in gratitude. ~